TRACE

ELEMENTS

ALSO BY BARBARA JORDAN

Channel

TRACE

ELEMENTS

Barbara Jordan

PENGUIN POETS

PENGUIN BOOKS
Published by the Penguin Group
Penguin Putnam Inc., 375 Hudson Street,
New York, New York 10014, U.S.A.
Penguin Books Ltd, 27 Wrights Lane,
London W8 5TZ, England
Penguin Books Australia Ltd, Ringwood,
Victoria, Australia
Penguin Books Canada Ltd, 10 Alcorn Avenue,
Toronto, Ontario, Canada M4V 3B2
Penguin Books (N.Z.) Ltd, 182–190 Wairau Road,
Auckland 10, New Zealand

Penguin Books Ltd, Registered Offices:
Harmondsworth, Middlesex, England

First published in Penguin Books 1998

3 5 7 9 10 8 6 4 2

LIBRARY OF CONGRESS CATALOGING IN PUBLICATION DATA
Jordan, Barbara, 1949–
Trace elements/Barbara Jordan.
p. cm.—(Penguin poets)
ISBN 0-14-026531-7
I. Title.
PS3560.067T73   1998
811'.54—dc21   97-34448

Printed in the United States of America
Set in Centaur MT
Designed by Claudyne Bedell

For Berg, many years a friend

ACKNOWLEDGMENTS

A section of "Edge," "The Cult of Solitude," and "Chernobyl" first appeared in *apex of the M*; "Hammond Pond" in *The Agni Review*; "Common Ephemeral" and "Crucible" in *Image: A Journal of Art and Religion*; "Dirt Road, Kilcoe, Cork" in *The New Criterion*; "Bud," "Walking to Rome," and "Fly Amanita" in *First Intensity*; "Formula" and "Anchorites" in *Ashen Meal*; "Spectrum" in *The Chicago Review*; "Threshold" in *The Atlantic Monthly*; "Elegy for Fireflies" and "Meander" in *Orion Magazine*; "O" in *notus*; "Menteth Glen" in *Harvard Review*; and "Ammonites" in *Seneca Review*.

I am grateful to fellowships from the National Endowment for the Arts, the Massachusetts Artists Foundation, and the Bread Loaf Writers' Conference.

Contents

PART I ⚜ EDGE

PART II ⚜ CRUCIBLE

PART III ❧ AMMONITES

TRACE

ELEMENTS

PART I

EDGE

EDGE

—FOR KALLIOPI N.

1.
Begin with debris, and let the wind carry you
into the early hours;
there everything meets, at last, some wall or gate,
the mandate of an unyielding obstacle.

This is the border of desire,
where the mountain, *keeping still,* rules the abyss,
and the moon always hovers, orange and full
at the end of the street. And you,

having gone to lock the car, stay
and look up—as if into a room seldom entered
            or thought of,
remote but familiar, an edifice
climbed by the pendulous blackness of trees,

the stammering chastity of stars. You want
to feed on its influence—this night that flows
            like a manta ray
over your life, that won't acknowledge
you tell it everything

and hold nothing back, even the indigestible
bones, the predator's confession—all mouth
and urgency.

2.
You stare, through nights of longing, at the sky
          outstaring you:
receptive to any projection—an impasse,
a luminous ruin, with its powers, principalities,
                    thrones—
like looking down a well
that's grievance-choked, clotted with the diadems
          of waterflowers,
with half-images stolen from Doré, a swirl
of movement into darkness (the Virgin standing
on the world, on a serpent
who churns into Draco, Scorpius, uroboros, Lucifer,
          bright star falling)

and falling,
among the iconographies of origin.

3.

What is memory but falling particles,
like sun-motes in a woods we cannot navigate,
but where tableaux, like wayside shrines, of mother
                    father, house
appear, intact amidst the footnotes and regrets,
the vegetation of our shadow-life.

Who gathers knowledge gathers pain, and stalks
            in mysteries
a palliative for unbelief,
while every compass points towards death, and

landscape flowers in the mind
outside of time—a replica of sun and moon,
            bulb and lily,
the ambiguity of a breeze shifting gestures
in the trees—such residues of mimicries
that seem parental.

4.
Leaning into the edge, you're seduced by the way
        it withdraws
behind the clouds, into the sky's drifting depths
like a river, or a door
as mysterious as the interior
of some museum sarcophagus, propped upright
        and enterable,
scrawled with signs—the blank eye of the sun,
an owl, a woman with her arms spread
over the night—signs you would read if you could
        read the past;
but a storm is blowing out of Paradise,
piling debris on debris, shifting the syntax
        indeterminably
(gilt and movement, leaves, upended chairs),
as if history were tumbling from a closet
you cannot
        cordon off
like a crime scene, in a room with no night-light,
where your heartbeat is the sound an insect makes
        tapping at glass
in the ruins of something never finished, or
once possible.

❖

There are no symbols in the world, only things
we tend, an integrity to imperfection.
From a height it would be pure blue: a small pond, almost
      round. Closer,
see how every stalk grows long in the tooth—pickerelweed
and iris lean into mud; and the carp blooming with fungus,
a day moon floating up
like another styrofoam cup in shallow water.
Along the banks, rugged marsh ferns circulate the air
      with slow uprisings,
willows shade the parking lot—and when the wind lifts
from tree to tree an exulting and silver-backed
      trembling starts,
as if something will be uncovered: a clue, a promise.

My father has walked at Hammond Pond for forty years.
As wilderness goes, a few miles of woods, dark and edged
      with muskrat holes;
it thins behind the mansions of Chestnut Hill
where rhododendrons suddenly block the path, and stacked
      shutters or bricks
mark the perimeter of someone's yard. We'd turn back
then, my brother and sister and I,
following him. He was looking for something indefinite—
a rare flower or red-tailed hawk embodied it—but
human life dismayed us: if we came across a recent
      campfire,
he might feel the char like a scout, to tell us
how long ago they'd left.

Last spring, when the ice thawed, they pulled a body
from the water: a man who'd fallen through in winter,
          no one around—but my father
remembered a hole one morning in the cold linen light.
It's years since we went with him to the pond:
silence widens into exile, and exile becomes a place
          that nothing human legislates—
day has authority, and night.
Gnat swarms and mosquitoes in the layered emptiness;
the shopping mall's reflection
where a muskrat scores her slow, v-shaped furrow
          over the blue-white surface,
and a lone walker stands in the licorice scent
of water lilies, hooked in their subtle dissipations.

The woods clutched in sweet smells recede
into carnality, the murmurous daybeds of mantis
        and bluebead lily.
A hawk stabs what he has vomited,
confirms the thing is dead before he lets it
fall. He rubs his beak
on the branch. Two mallards roam a fishpond's
        green cartouche.

The shimmer of water, the arches of sky
provoke the childish urge to fly—
to cast off the mantle of *boy* or *girl* for unknown
        assignations—
to be ruthless in freedom. One summer day
when my grandmother was young, she said
an eagle snatched a living baby
from a field in Ireland. And we imagined
what happened.

Where on earth can awe cast a shadow now?
Compliantly, the trees lower their oars
        to a gust of wind;
the hawk adjusts his perch—
but the perspective's changed, and all seems
belittled, human-sized: the mirror has no depth.
What's unseen is merely a fable to us,
a pair of thorny wings, poised
over paradise.

COMMON EPHEMERAL

Rising and going downstairs, forgetting
why, the purpose lost
in that soft gauntlet of descent,
I step into groundlessness
again, as in dreams where I fly through high-
         ceilinged rooms,
the vast inchoate space of my repose.

And then I'm standing simply at the window,
foraging in trees: two sparrows
in a lilac bush: my consciousness
a replica of what I see,
my silence, an usher's.

I've watched an ant carry, the equivalent
of miles, its small burden
like an unformed thought—some casket
of dreams, mythical imago, pupa
the shape of an effigy. I've knelt, and put
            twigs across
its path, a gesture meant to interact,

or perhaps, to imitate the quiet strokes
that come out of the blue, and cloud
where I was going,
what I meant to do.

Some say that what we think is clear
has clearer form somewhere
in air, and its brightness attracts us;

but I'm unsettled, like a mayfly
who sees a shadow in a pond, and leaves
        uprising
absence in its wake, this vatic stare.

Your farm had been by the sea, that was all
you said of it. And here were trees and fuchsia
hedges, the sea elusive—
much closer than this, it seemed from the hill—
then invisible again. Alongside, a stream
shaded by plants that wouldn't thrive in brine:
willowy, but with stamina for winds,
and thickets that smelled of salt, sifting the krill
            of insect life,
pipits and sedge warblers, the summer pollens.
As I coasted fast on my bike, a pure white bird—
an egret or heron?—struck out from the water, legs
            slack, its wings
pumping downstream, into the intricate greenness.
I braked, my neck thrust out
in the same stunned momentum as the thing
I'd ambushed. Then silence, a sediment of wonder.
Did you live *here* and hardly speak of it?
I'd followed your sparse guidance, one sentence
            that unravelled
over farms by the sea in Kilcoe;
then I found the sea, cornflower blue, at the end
of a pasture that I crossed: a castle
on the headland, its upper rooms fluent with grass
the wind blew unremittingly.

Impending thoughtfulness. The weight of it
sustained by a calm vicinity
where hundred-year-old linden trees shade me
   in their coolness,
nobility of silence—the far, blue umbilicus
of sky.   What can we know, or find?
(The boy Saint Francis in the dark, asking over
   and over,
My God, What art Thou and what am I?—
there are many ways to ask it.)

But to make room for silence is difficult,
like letting a fire go out in the dark
when we fear the dark, and the leaves' soft
   agitations
become extensions of our own.

Loneliness is that small necklace of wind
touching my neck: the distance a language
   overlapping
with nuance, with things pronouncing themselves
as shifts and pressure on a web that stretches out
      beyond the treetops
to some invisible, distant heart.
For this, a child will leave mother and father
and cling to one small center
of self—predatory, so humanly vigilant,
knowing only what it is

by what it is not—that emphatic emptiness
above the corridors of leaves, that reflecting pool
of sky, from which a spider's trailing sentence
            drops a thread
into the mind,
and we compose the story of ourselves
in time: a falling from a higher ground
into gravity.

BUD

I remember, no, imagine
cochineal,
the purple of the murex snail,
a royal bee's

solitary flight, the fragrance
of an April night
half-formed,
a breast of moon:

and *puer* and *puella* summoned home
separately, in spider-light
to bed,
and wishing wells of shadows

in the room, the familiar
read as strange: the epicenter
of desire,
the cargo of innocence.

FORMULA

In every discussion of metaphysics
there must be a bit of silver
work in the background—and rain
suggesting stealth—for secrets spawn
          rumors,
while logic, mimicking the world, looks for
the straightest path to a formal center
as French gardens are arranged: a statue
          for a pivot
or the fountain we are hazy shadows in;
for it's the trappings which make the
subject romantic, elevated, or grave—
a wooden table, a skull, a window that
reveals the four elements composed in
pastoral symmetry like a postcard
of Paradise—symbols that say
thought is a window too, and you, the on-
looker, may examine a loony magnification
of details and come away
satisfied that *something* has been apprehended
if only a refocusing of components
which belong together in that room
we may call an altar:
a chalice, the sliding doors, the night
looming over marble.

ANCHORITES

Often, after death, the body of the contemplative
was sealed into his cell.
—HERMITS AND ANCHORITES OF ENGLAND

Imagine a hive made of stones. Then imagine
that one cell would be your tomb—
no different from a wasp's mud-daubed comb that falls
          from the eaves—
that you would not emerge.

The window draws me. The one the spider
looks through; the one that holds the saint in its
          hemisphere of light,
through which the town is visible,
and hills sprouting bushes, and the mild, arrested
commerce of clouds.

How much pressure the world exerts, though some
gaze the other way. Still, seasons fan or wither,
          mock constancy,
and yet affirm the building up and tearing down
of what we know afresh,
violets in dry riverbeds. Those oratories by the sea

seem like ghost-skulls, wind for a tongue,
where such men lived.
Their days turned inward, and the years unravelled
          every memory
of wandering: the flesh became wilderness
enough—Christ's outstretched arms to guide them

through the dark, where desires grow devious.
Tonight I kneel
by my window, under stars like the tiny teeth of a
        grass snake,
wondering how to contemplate
their lives, who made a nest of emptiness.

The silence furthers, and the night is full
of ambient light, a mossy darkness
that encloses thoughts
there's nectar in—the scent of linden trees
      carried downwind,
these watermarks of stars.
How sweet life is when it's clear
of uneasiness, the crescent edge of something
flashing in a cloudy pond, the spawn
of anxious gestures

I escape awhile, standing alone outside
the gate of who I am, dreaming where the river
      goes:
time only an iris open or closed,
an interval a cloud passing the moon. There,
at the end of visible light, estuaries
vanish into a trace—
indigo-violet's the barrier reef
no human eye penetrates.

My white dog lies on the grass and works a bone;
her teeth scraping marrow is the only sound.

Distance is at bay, and emptiness has gone
where emptiness goes:
into the arches of morning, wordlessly
back to its distillates
before myth, even before Adam
                    named the serpent and the bee,
said *fox*, and *wood thrush*, and glimpsed
the fact of yes and no
in an elemental light—that knowledge
differentiates, requires separation

as a painting needs perspective,
else lion and lamb float beside the child
enlarged beyond proportion—
for each must reckon with a horizon
conceived as endpoint, a kind of teleology
                    of matter.
But by innocent distortion
memory will coincide the parts
into a whole—insubstantial, primitive
        as Eden—
everything equal, having been gathered
from some rib of thought
extending its imaginary line back
to what was, is, and not.

THRESHOLD

—FOR DOUG EATON

How the day turns in the westerly woods.
Not a gust.
A gold, fastidious light slides waist-deep
and ascends through the trees
as the mercury drops. We discern,
among the hierarchies of branch and cloud,
the circle we inhabit—open-roofed, visited
          by owls—
and imagine ourselves watched from above.
Precarious radiance
frames the skylit world, the soft catkins
that hang from the alders. We sit at the edge
          of stillness,
and a few frogs begin to call, one to another,
with a ragged scintillance
in the whiteness of water at dusk: blue-
white, except where the shadows stipulate.
Look, there are stepping-stones;
I think our minds hold nothing but this world
          reflected,
and we can cross above the early stars
into the mantle of the pine woods—
our hands and faces luminous in the bending
          darkness—
vulnerable as a summer porch the moths get in,
the door ajar.

PART II

CRUCIBLE

Those who renounce explosions, once and for all, forever—where can they withdraw to?

There is no forest left for the hermits, and the rice in the begging bowl is poisoned.

—ELIAS CANETTI, THE SECRET HEART OF THE CLOCK

CRUCIBLE

Tonight, a faint metallic odor falls
with the rain over Cracow, where statues
in the courtyard of St. Peter and Paul
lapse beyond redemption, their features
pocked by chemicals. Over Prague,
a purple smudge of sunset, a soot pollen
spreads a grave radiance across the sky.
Lead, sulfur dioxide, mercury
foul the narrow Street of the Alchemists,
the Hradcany castle, the whole gold-gray
sea-fed alembic of air currents.
        The winds blow east.
On the mountain borders, dead and stunted trees
seem a portcullis of conifers and oaks.
In village after village lung disease
and solemnness, the brown haze of coal smoke
from burning lignite.
        Underground, in mines
that once produced uranium or salt,
the sick rest and spend the daylight breathing
better air. Strange sanatoriums
for children, these places, with crystal
and beryl in the walls, rumors of dwarfs.
        (In poetry,
the most poisonous things can sound lovely,
as in the old recipes: *aqua fortis,*
butter of antimony, gas sylvestris—)
And, as in stories, there were premonitions
in the weather, calves stillborn, roses
and plum trees with misshapen blossoms.
Songbirds disappeared. People carried

the Black Madonna through the land, draped
in silver robes, a crown of stars; everyone
prayed for miracles. We've changed earth to fire
       and fire to air
beyond reckoning, and find regret
hard to measure. The eruption of Krakatoa
(dust now in memory, legendary cloud)
took three years to dissipate, but sunset
and dawn, they say, were beautiful
the world over.

WALKING TO ROME

—FOR GERALD BURNS

Copper blue and ash disband and combine
to make a sky, or else whiteness weighs down
the suburbs and woodland Constable loved
as pedestals for clouds. We move on, beneath

a penitentiary dusk, where the pressure
of heaven over matter leaves no room
to intervene an imaginary line, or
an arching brightness through the trees that some

mistake for purpose—the stillborn dream
of enlightenment, knowledge—like woodsmoke
in the distance; and, beyond that, ruins, a hard-
        edged sublime,
the auspice of seagulls. So we turn, back

to gold-leafed skies, anonymous
hermit scenes, the horizon scattered with beasts
        and marble tombs,
fruit glowing in half-light by a cottage door—
another *Rest on the Flight* or *St. Jerome*,

the division between here and there
without true perspective, both close and far.

ELEGY FOR FIREFLIES

Hikers come upon these ruins
untroubled by tourists, the one fountain that still pours
into a basin of sky.
The old entablatures have worn away: a frieze
of tribute? gods? ears of corn?
Here a hand raised, it seems, in blessing—
or a branch. And small companion symbols scattered
            in a sunburst,
like minnows when you drop a rock in water.

Others have gleaned the useful rubble and left us
a kind of shell game to imagine
what it was. We picked up shards, faintly riddled,
as if birds had walked on soft mud. A temple,
or a prosperous monastery,
though it might have been a Roman merchant's house.

Nor can we know, for certain, how the terrain looked
before now. There are places on the Peloponnesus—
barren hills with wisps of grass—where long ago
thick oak forests grew,
for there must have been trees for Athena's owls,
            and for the mysteries,
and laurels, and pines to make a thyrsus. And once
wolves foraged an evacuated Rome—it is said
Belisarius, entering at night with his army, mistook
            their eyes
for distant torchlights.

A few fireflies flicker here between the branches.
Bee-starred ones, little droplets of platinum,
let the dark not swallow you for good:
that river runs through everything, waist-high
            and tree-high
made of wind—
through the backyards and the train tracks,
in the ditches by the highways.

O

The circling a hawk makes
is a question. Over and over,
a branch bends to touch its
shadow, the world
obstacle and no obstacle.
At ebb, the sky's a far-off
mohair blue, a cabinet

of clouds. Meteors will fall
tonight, from a spot
in the northeastern horizon
near Perseus. Each year
we orbit through this
veil of debris; each month
an apothecary moon,

our old hunting companion,
follows us through the fields.
Quartz, round rocks,
fossils from an inland sea
drop into pockets—
one more for the collection

heap. And small bones
under the tallest tree
the hawk cast off
will dissolve to carbon
again, the leaves turn,
another ring form.

URBAN SETTING

I know the temperament of what we own:
the bureau with its hemisphere of light;

the bedlamp's Grecian scene, faint ormolu;
and Bacon's portrait of the poet Blake,

his features drawn like silk over pearskin,
the petulance of his death mask, composed

in a sea of black, the way my own face
looks back from the window like a ghost

bathed by the glow of the computer's screen
where tiny planets, moons, and suns

are casting spores of light across a space
as passive as the sky at night—or someone

keeping vigil with discontent, staring
at things she can't articulate;

and pain is far away, it is my satellite.

SUB ROSA

Who knew you'd been dreaming of escape
all winter, building a careful way out
of love's complexities—the secret stair

resurrected, as prisoners do, board
by board—into the future. And how
irredeemably sweet to break on through

to another side, regardless
love. For me,
the nights are obstacles, and morning
expands on emptiness, the here

and there of living apart, impossible
simultaneity of any sky. Sometimes, I want
            to climb after you,
as if that stair could have held us both
suspended, refusing to grow old.

1.
Shadows lengthen and touch
behind me, where our voices gloss
sun-shafted rooms, the city echoing
below us—shouts, heel-taps—late spring
nights, the smell of greenness blowing
from new leaves, half-open
like butterflies drying. And we'd sleep
that way, side by side—although often,
       waking in the dark,
I'd slip to the window, that sweetness
lifting me . . . translunary,
already looking back
to see the shape of my life being lived
beside you.
Now, each backward glance ignites
fresh pain.

2.

I keep what I've lost, the past being
a kind of compass,

a place where the light will hold
its breath.

And today climbs toward uncertainty,
deciduous moods that leaf

and regret.
I walk in the woods. I get over you.

A burled stick becomes a talisman
for an afternoon, lost among many

sequestered now. A light snow, deer tracks
into wordless places—no memory

has currency here. Flying off, a crow veers
to look at me:

I'm only a woman
holding a broken branch.

It's dusk, twilight, or dawn
in the forest—
the corridor merely a path from which, right or left,
        we see a clearing—
light fanning out from a stem of moon,
silhouettes of trees,
a quietness implicit behind glass, where

as in a dream, animals take no notice
although we look into their dens, and down
        a shallow stream
that mirrors a gray-violet sky,
while they feed on dusty leaves, or sleep
in loose familial groups, and we pretend
the scene is real
but wonder by what means they were killed

that left no marks on their pelts—preserved
for years—and how their eyes require
special irises, sheeted glints of gold or amber
        spokes—
made in a special factory, perhaps
by a woman with a wolf's photograph
above her bench, painting them in small strokes,
like brushing luminescent numerals on a clock

when they used radium to make them glow
in the dark, like the rosaries I took into the closet
as a child, hand-cupping the beads to see them
        coiled

pale green, the krypton of another world
that conjured X-rays, bones, the atomic bomb
I would survive,
finding my way by the wattage of my will

through strange and empty streets
without butterflies or mothers,
like being lost in a museum, having stalled
          at some detail—
clouds captured in a puddle,
a songbird somehow perched askew—
while others have moved on, familiar coats
trailing off into other rooms.

CHERNOBYL

No one there (already dying) believed it:
the roof open to the stars, the blow
to the skull, nor the phosphorescent cloud
lifting out over the marshes, beyond
the remedy of words.
                                        It must have seemed
that something holy was escaping;
there is no sanctuary
when meaning dislocates, when terror moves
exponentially (nothing and everything
out of place), and any night becomes a locked room,
            a map of shadows,
luminous dials, the glass of water by the bed.

(And while we sleep, the hours drop their dust;
the angel passes by our house, stops elsewhere.)

So sequence unfolds to consequence
as faithfully as wind, as the low-pressure zones
we watch, omnisciently, swirling west to east
            on a planetary chart;
and like gods we pity, remotely,
those whose death will come in a cloud—
for we are (admit it) hungry for flames, the world
            as witness
to its own ends. We lift up, fitfully, our hearts.
Catastrophe is revelation of a kind.

RESIDUAL MATTER

—FOR STEPHEN ATHERTON

Anything is a point of departure
if you wish: another entrance
to uncertainty, the drifting pressure of lists
            and more lists
like stepping-stones you put down to cross
out to some quiet place—not here,
but somewhere

always out of reach (too early, too far),
composed as a prospect
of sky and hills, a marginal attentiveness
            you'll sense
will happen, as one can read the knowing
eye on a rose's stem, seeing there the green
                        premonition
of a branch.
And to stare into the stare
that moment extends, to lift your head

as for a kiss, and accept
you are weary—like a hunter who at last lies down
            in the long expanse of pursuit—
finding the rest
was preparation, illusion, entanglements
of matter: the path sorrow and desire make

dimensional, through the burgeoning
indifference of things.

If it were possible to cultivate
an austere astonishment, they did. Dark panels
of, say, a stag's head, lemons on a silver dish,
        and roses:
the incongruities of hunt and harvest, additions
of this, and this, and this
were what wealth was—stunned opulence, a dreamy
        trout's eye
upturned with golden flecks, the offhand glimpse
of pelts hung on a storeroom peg,
culinary dishabille.

Was it a bourgeois fantasy—
so much to put away, leave it in a heap—
or were painters dazzled by the overlay
of Chinese porcelain, barbarous fruits, damask
        and peonies
sharing the table with a tethered boar?
Or, is every still life a savoring of what's out there,
just embellished versions
of the bison walls at Lascaux:
something to wish for, of imposing possibility?

VIPER LIGHT

Dampness, and things drift out of focus
in the hampering not-quite-dark:
a calla lily's 40-watt
softness downhill, elect over shadowy hosta.

Odd, as the light withdraws, how I grow
more distinctly incarnate:
an instrument of touch, vulnerable to the obstacles
that each step supposes—

branches hung low, the quarrels of roots.
Often I stop,
like a listener at a keyhole, feeling the wind
examine an ankle or wrist, sensing

the tiny exhalations I'm surrounded by.
Glints. The clicks of twigs.
I look up at a sky
that falls miraculously close, and step through

a casement of vines,
tapping the ground as I would going downstairs
in the dark, vertigo of unknowing
into the cluttered world and its subterfuge.

WHAT OPENS

—FOR ELAINE

I'd like to believe in angels, but a blue heron
will do, or that willow with its feathery leaves—
for who has seen an angel? Or, seeing one,
who can name the species—say it is the rarest
        of seraphim,
or declare it nocturnal, a light-bearer,
its wings powdery with matter like a moth's?

One summer in the Berkshires, I saw
a creature hovering and uncurling its long tongue
        inside a flower.
A tiger lily. And a hawk moth. It was dusk,
before the fireflies kindle their flickering
        messages,
when the edges of things reciprocate,
and our eyes adjust to the staves and cups
and whiffs of blackness—

as if attention might delay the fleeting
presence, as the dying are said to waiver when
        called to—
because what fades in time, fades in us.
Yet you say you saw two angels, not two men,
step from mist and low clouds and greet you
on a lonely stretch of beach;
and you were certain

for no rational reason. Perhaps what
opens always closes after us, the link as tenuous
          as moth's tongue
to lily stamen, as that impending darkness
we distinguish beneath the rectitude
of birdsong. We need consolation, its bewildering
          nectar;
and what is it they tell us, anyway?
Go in peace, they say, *Do not be afraid.*

PART III

AMMONITES

1.
Our words trail out of matter
to other versions. The silence shades,
now and then, innocent deceptions:
a deer's nervous spoor along the stream bed,
or, if we lift these branches—
such purple lilies sweetening at the water's
        edge,
rafters of bees in a willow,
auroral, unsettling shifts of attention
when the sun unclouds.
I was thinking of what Fenollosa said,
that a sentence in nature is a stroke of lightning,
the verbal energy carried from sky
to ground; and even a change of wind can
abduct my imagination—
serene, dispirited, turning small bones in memory's
        grate,
undoing, trying to formulate
new hybrids from old configurations,
waving a bothersome insect away with a leaf
I broke off.

2.

Our words trail out of matter, where once
animal tracks were noun
and verb: the marginalia of exit and return,
everything circling
a secret place.
(Do you remember the elephant graveyard, Tarzan
          privileged to be led there?)
Instinct as ritual in brute creatures: blue flowers
strewn in Neanderthal graves, and the lion's teeth
a handful of fierce seeds
not for scattering, but kept. Emerging distance
hermetical
the gatekeeper-animal faces carved,   a bird
          calling all the light
from the snow;
webworks of trees, scents, familiar debris—

3.
Consciousness as landscape,
Augustine was mindful of it. "The caverns of memory,"
 he wrote,
"the mountains and hills of my high imagination."
Heaven overhead, and deep in the earth glimmers
and beryls, termites
threading the forest into their tunnels.
Was the aqueduct a paradigm for grace, are there
pivots into abstraction?

Lost cities in our heads, the agar of ghosts,
with sea-winds and forlorn skies
arouse when we walk alone—remembering Schliemann
sending the workers home at the first, quick
 · glint—
scanning the ground for some rare thing:
(weathered stick shaped like a fox's head, vaguely,
means what?)
nothing. Gold sunset,
mica, quartz, flint and leaves, a dead beetle dried
 by the sun, kept—
what we hoard decorates our fears
as Egyptians would protect the ka. The morphology
of mystery in a curio cabinet, the wildness
brought indoors, to have a mind
like Goethe's study.

4.
How far back the silence goes
into the cave mouth.
There are steps we follow, and places
with no markers. And if, at the edge of a clearing
we should chance to see a deer
tethered to her shadow, her tracks already filling
            with light—
will memory wrap that living image
as tenderly as stone
held an archaeopteryx in its final shrug: the head
            and neck lowered,
and the feathers under its wings like fern fronds?

❧

FLY AMANITA

There was a false bottom to the season,
and bees slept, clinging, on the zinnias,
caught by the chill
of late afternoon, the sky blue as a geode.
And yet the wind is soft, the way curtains
soothe me when I'm ill, and out and in
are all that matter. Sun or shade, this

teaspoon of rain on a leaf.
What is it we know and then unknow?
The season folding back upon itself—
grief, self-pity, wisdom?
I've been living in one room with poetry:
the world shrunk to a word,
and the page a map, where bee and boulder

are as moveable as true and false,
and every path will stray into the past
if I let it. How often I've followed
wistfulness with its purple smoke,
clung to its estranged certainty
as to some murky *cogito*, and stumbled
over branches of pine or oak

under trees where the fly amanita grows,
touchable, but poisonous.

MENTETH GLEN

—FOR DONNA RICHARDSON

It wandered the way imagination
wanders the path on a Chinese mountain
that fits in your hand.
Under a ledge of trees, from the clay gray
shale, we pried up brachiopods—small
        Devonian shells—
still moist from the stream bed, perfectly
ridged and winged, and corals,
though we were a star's age
from the sea they'd lived in, in a place
where the light turned as bright as spent
        cartridges.

I remember those drawings of early life,
"Swamp Forest of the Carboniferous Age,"
or "Silurian Coral Reef,"
that kept me hours in my room.
Even a child understands time as a tree
        laden with rumors,
its crown in bloom, a flying reptile perched
in its deadwood—and who hasn't stepped
into the chamber of a great tree with names
        and years
carved on it? I thought of Jonson

standing under Sidney's oak at Penshurst,
the same stippled veil of leaves, and the rest
        adumbration;
of Shelley's *Defense*, that poetry is

"consummate surface and bloom of all things";
how texture inclines us to look closer.
All day, we stooped in and out of shadows,
and time was a terrace that followed the path
        of water,
a gap of sky we entered, dislodging stones.

Breathing deep at the open window. Narcissi
and winter roses on the sill, the snow
outside freezing mollusk-hard.
On my wall, two carnivores battle
before the ubiquitous volcano, "On a Cretaceous
          landscape,"
the caption reads, "in what is now New Jersey."

Bison-like, coated with snow, a few cars
coast from the buxom silence
down Boylston Street. And I fall, suddenly,
through some crevice of doubt
where fears take shape, prehistoric and
          changeless,
in the burrowing moonlight.

"The actual landscape with its actual horns"
is stranger than conjecture.
I've heard how museums misplaced the ribs
on their skeletons, expanding the thorax
          under a fossil hull—
so they'd move, if they could, unnaturally
teetering. Linnaeus classified them

with the mineral kingdom, as stones.
The first finds of paleontology
were pulverized for cures, hunted in biblical
          passages:
dragons' teeth, unicorns, basilisk bones;

though Aristotle said that species
were immutable, eternal as the earth

where things rise and decay. Elemental
mixtures of form: the narcissi, the snow,
my fingers with their unprecedented whorls—
          variations
in matter, when what matters will not stay
one shape. I lean out to gauge
the known, referential world, a hall of exits.

MEANWHILE

Between the air and airless stars
a region of indifference
confines us to our consciences, and paths
that wind from villages
into each uneven, arbitrary day.

Again and back the same desire
divides the distance, distantly
as if it sought a temporal thing—
autumn gives way to tears;
bees wander softly through low trees,

and heaven shakes its tenantry
of emptiness, of love.

Let the form be a garden in wild wilderness,
a hyacinth language, a turning in wind
         when marginal influences
disrupt the flow.

Build thought as a bee does,
one concern at a time, a hexagonal symmetry
         deep in the structure;
or explore the foundation

of a derelict house, its cellarhole cracked
by bracken and trees—with daffodils blooming
         alongside the door,
and off in the woods, sometimes

a forsythia. And a carrion beetle to bury
the mouse, the skeletal memories of things
         that are gone;
or hidden, like antlers, deep in the pines

where branches are tossed,
a path to the edge of recorded time, that stops
         at a place
where the language is lost.

I was lured by the cupboard darkness
of recesses, the vigil lights that flickered
in the leaves, and animal furrows that pressed
into ferns and thickets for the hinges
of the forest. A place to sit, timeless,
moth-still child hiding under the bushes
thinking God couldn't see, who would poke
a spider's web, do something wicked.
         Birdcalls tapped holes
in the silence, so it breathed, like the jars
I trapped butterflies in with a flower,
the illusion of treasures—which, released, flew off
like disoriented prayers. I found them
floating, symbolizing the soul,
through the still lifes of Otto van Schrieck:
always of shady woods, a lizard or snake
(lurid, camouflaged) waiting to strike,
while we see the drama from the ground
level—as if perched on a dew-cup,
a human tribunal.

Quaint, now, to see in nature *tenebrae*
and *lux*, beyond the vagaries of cumulus,
the irises a breeze lifts into sheafs
of raw, blue nerves. It is aberrant beauty
we pursue—the light of fairy tales so close
        to grace,
Magritte's twilight with the shadows wrong,
as if the root of sacred, "set apart,"
were tangible in some primeval place.

It seemed through mythic archways, or in dreams,
they might estimate the proportions of Paradise:
            innocence a state of
looking back,
nothing untouched or unassessed; they entered

the wilderness, rank with trophies; nailed names
on the tree trunks—genus and species
to guide them through Genesis—
the apple, Malus malus, so called by Linnaeus

from the root, evil.

AMMONITES

In Goethe's house they'd roped the rooms to keep us
moving in predetermined ways.

In Goethe's house, a hundred cabinets for specimens
in drawers as narrow as they make
for dental instruments. Catalogues of minerals,
crystals, bones, the fossil fronds of tiny ferns,
          insects in amber, flint—
and freestanding gods and satyrs,
amethysts, imprints left in shale,
and one huge ammonite, a foot across—and some
were bored, discreetly, and firmly bolted down.

The study, like a chapel in mild sun, was quiet
and untrespassed, neutral as agar
with everything put away—the glinting calipers,
          microscopes, distilling jars.
Now begonias on the sill, a table set for two
for visitors to imagine his ghost
with a friend—with Schiller perhaps, disputing
Linnaeus, or undoing the convoluted tenderness
          of ligament and vine
to see the inner thing,
the moving mandible; talking poetry.

We bought postcards. Of the study, of his deathbed,
and of a four-foot Hera's head on a pedestal
photographed, on a starry night, beside an open window.

❖

A block from Goethe's house, a woman was selling
fossils, ammonites mostly, formed so long ago
that they defied comprehension,
though I tried, holding them gravely, like a psychic
            would a pocket watch.
200,000,000 years and still articulate,
ammonite ceratites evolutus, a kind of nautilus,
            tightly coiled,
each whorl embracing earlier ones, distinctive
sutures marking its growth.

So an increment of time evolves in the mind's
            abstracting eye
to one amorphous image seen from a height
and shaped by what prevailed—
a smattering of banners and turrets, whole centuries
condensed to a few pillars.
And we extrapolate from a fossil shell

that Weimar was, once, an inland sea.
The woman said, for ammonites, we could look
            on a mountain nearby,
and I remembered, behind the house, Goethe's
spindly coach, black and gold, like a great mosquito
with its shaft sunk in cobblestones,
how he'd driven through these foothills, that here
was a trail we might follow, a connection

sought, as if by the laws of magic—sympathy
and contagion—to touch what has been touched,
to walk the same ground,
to add the self to an equation. 200,000,000 years,
          people, stars,
and each individual, anywhere a pilgrimage.
We should look, she told us, *under the memorial,*
on Buchenwaldberg.

It means beech-forest-mountain. A vestigial, offhand name,
grown clenched and darker than the woods,

long gone, that might have grown. We avoided thoughts
but ammonites, our eyes lowered under the lintel

of sunset, climbing up a rutted road to corrugated fields,
scanning stones, everywhere the ground eroded

where Russian tanks had practiced war before the Wall
came down. Now nothing on this side but the memorial

rising like a concrete water tower; on the other side
the camp, unseen, imagined topographically as chalk-pit

or mire, quicksand to any mind that reaches for
the remote, preemptory branch. An ankle-twisting hole

contains an old patent bottle, blue-tinged and pale
as the sky: *Lebensessenz* written in glass—

essence of life—and inside, stoppered with a bit of moss,
a clump of earth. How easily we believe

in what we want: some substance to transform our lives,
a future entered through an arch

where every heightened step revives old dreams.
From where we stood, it seemed we could look back

at evil, as at something we'd outgrown—that years
had swept the landscape clean—or rather

we were facing west, and took the full brunt
of the light upon ourselves, who, like the mountain

decline a shadow side.

*Memorial. Turn the word on your tongue and feel
its core—the bit of death in it, prolonged
in chiseled stone. A landmark you pass on the way
          to somewhere,
to walk around and feel. Unreal
as memories dredged up from the vantage of a hill at
          sunset—
the distance calling to the distant—and the answer,
to go home.*

An ammonite centered on the mantel,
a small sky-blue bottle beside it, and some lilacs
        from the garden
construe a narrative of sorts, however private
the frame of meaning, there
at some intersection of things—the world being
        subject
to judgment, to contingencies, to the abyss

between trash and keepsake. And yet do I
relegate as commonplace
souvenirs or bric-a-brac the things I've found
        impenetrable;
manipulate aesthetically
these auras impossible to excavate—the burden
unshouldered, but put down as proof

regarding itself: knowledge

the tree to which grief and loss are nailed
and then forgotten, burrowed
in the vast softness of morning. *Everything
        is leaf*—
Goethe wrote from Italy—*root, stem, and blossom,*
        a metamorphic botany

unfolding from the first progenitor,
then named again, hierarchically,
as the Tribes, Nations, and Families of things—

the *patrician* lilies, "adorning the vegetable kingdom
        with the splendor of courts,"
the *servile* mosses and *plebeian* grasses
which, "the more they are taxed and trod upon,
the more they multiply"—distinctions

as murky as any investment:
say, a tiny bear hand-painted on a beech-tree leaf,
or a snip of hair in a specimen box
by Joseph Bueys, shaman of dislocated things,
        of taxonomy gone awry,
who'd kept a copy of Linnaeus's *Systema Naturae*
he'd pulled from a bonfire
as a child at Hitler Youth. He would have known

of a church in Cologne
with a room called *der goldene Kammer,*
the golden chamber, whose walls, dimly lit, seem
        encrusted with shells,
but they're human, ribs and femurs that spell,
in lettered bones, prayers in Latin. What is art but
        the wish
to make strategies of design? Everywhere the ground

eroded at some intersection of knowing, disordered
as a room of impaled moths, butterflies
dustless under glass, coffee cups, wings, thoraxes,
        a dictionary

opened to ammonites—the root "Ammon's horn,"
their coils resembling a ram's, an animal sacred
          to Jupiter-Ammon,
or to Ammon-Ra—the accounts differ,

one thing referring to another.

BARBARA JORDAN received her B.A. from Harvard University and an M.A. from Boston University. Her first book, *Channel*, won the Barnard New Women Poets Prize. She has received awards from the National Endowment for the Arts and from the Massachusetts Artists Foundation, and she has been a fellow at the Bread Loaf Writers' Conference and a recipient of the Grolier Poetry Prize. Her poems have appeared in *The Atlantic*, *The New Yorker*, *Sulfur*, *The New Criterion*, *The Paris Review*, and other magazines. She lives in upstate New York and is an associate professor of English at the University of Rochester, where she teaches creative writing.

PENGUIN POETS